The Butterfly will Rise

EMILY BARRUS

The Butterfly will Rise

Copyright @ 2024, by Emily Barrus

ISBN: 979-8-218-35952-2

Printed in the United States of America

Books by Emily Barrus

Breathe

God's Got This

In Loving Memory of

Grandmalita

A poem she originally wrote in Spanish:

The past leaves us in prints.

Happy moments we shared and enjoyed.

I hope these moments won't ever be erased as

the camel prints in the desert are erased by the wind.

These moments should stay strong...

like a memory that is not easy to erase,

that remains...

And still lives in the life that will come.

11/19/1952 – Pinalejo, Honduras

Words won't slow me down
you were with me for all
of my yesterdays,
I set you free
like a caged bird,
you won't see my tomorrows
I will rise without you to
unknown heights,
watch me soar,
giving up is not in my
vocabulary

I dread the rain
the dark, murky clouds roll in
Why detest something that
will help me grow?
The storm is merely
passing through

A sunset is the sweetest goodbye

the sun gives every night

Hope is here

in the in-between moments

it's still here amidst

the worries

somedays,

it may be harder to find,

don't lose heart,

look closely,

hope is here

5

Last night was unbearable,

I had almost lost hope in

humanity, until I remembered

God is still on the throne,

His plan is perfect,

no matter what may

be thrown my way

if I choose to keep on

He can use me…

…will I let Him use me?

A sunrise is a sign of a fresh start.

It's not your fault,

no matter how much

the devil whispers deceit

with Christ, you have the

power to stand and fight

against your greatest enemy,

let Christ set you free

from the bonds of fear

and doubt

A dead butterfly may seem
deeply depressing,
but I can't help thinking
of the life it lived
the smiles and hopeful wonder
it gave just flying by
you may not know the difference
you are making,
but believe me
you are making one

I have finally found peace,

I thought that might take

my whole life to say,

I am fighting the fight,

I am running the race,

I am ready for what comes next

One step at a time
is all it takes,
no one should make you move
faster, if you're not ready
it can make you or break you,
which do you choose?

She stood at the water's edge

staring, dreaming

she walked into the rolling waves

eager to wash her tears away,

she didn't ask for this

and yet she was here

determined to make the best

of what life gave her

Dreams are not just fun
escapes from reality,
sometimes they are secrets
hidden deep within us,
we may keep them buried
until it's too late,
I beg of you, please don't
the world needs you
to go after your dreams,
you never know how you
can change the world
until you try

You can be brave

here in these moments

of uncertainty,

in fact,

your soul depends on it

Peace and love,
it's not just a flowery
sign in the Miami airport,
it's what we should live with
every day
for the rest of our lives

You push me aside

not caring for how I feel

or maybe you never knew

and that's why it hurts so much

I am still here

alive and well

I'm not meant to be

cast aside

for if you continue down this path,

you may also be forgotten

You are here on this day

in this exact moment for a reason

don't lose hope,

storms will rage,

fear and doubt

may hold you close,

let your inner courage

from deep within

rise up,

never let it go,

keep looking forward,

the best is yet to come

The resilience of flowers

amazes me,

even after the harshest winters,

they push through the

soil and bloom

cascading happiness and

hope to whoever

passes by,

sadness fades,

hope lingers

Fall is here
the crunching of leaves
under every step,
some may feel sadness
wash over them,
during this season,
some may feel hope,
spring always follows
fall and winter,
while spring may feel far off,
it's coming,
a fresh start is waiting for you,
you must simply begin

I thought I had to have

perfect words for you

and yet, I didn't

I thought you wanted

my heart's musings

and yet you didn't,

the world has stopped

it's waiting for us to

make up our minds

there's no time to waste

Here in these empty moments,
Jesus is here
even if it doesn't feel like it,
our bodies may grow
weary and thin
during this thing called life,
but hold fast,
don't lose hope,
Jesus is coming again

The world hates
I give in and hate back

The world loves
I give in and love back

The world has consumed me
and I've consumed it

Death was upon me now
there was nothing I could
do to stop it.

It was looming above me

Tears flow from an endless vase

I know not from where they come

my soul has fought

through many a storm,

I am afraid this is only the

beginning,

my strength to keep on

has dried up,

I don't know what to do

Silence is requested
to let my soul breathe,
it whispers my darkest
thoughts and my bravest dreams,
I never know what it is going
to tell me next,
I wait for the silence,
and it waits for me

25

I fret for all my todays
and tomorrows,
what else is there?
I am all but a skeleton
waiting for death
to come rescue me

God brought me to this place
of hope and unconditional love,
I am nothing without Him,
I yearn to be near Him
night and day,
He is all that I have

Hope shalt not come
for there is no one to help me,
I've prayed in earnest
and yet still waiting on an
answer,
shall I keep trying, or shall
I give up?

You are but a bitter memory
from a time not too long ago,
things were said
and I was misled,

I can never be rid of you,
no matter how hard I try,
you are tattooed on my soul

You rip your heart out at the sight of me,

you say I disgust you,

you say beauty is vain,

and yet you hate me,

you thought I was mad

for doing such a thing,

I only did it in an attempt

to be rid of you

Love me not for all of my

todays and tomorrows,

but for the here and now

we only have but this moment,

the next is not guaranteed,

come away with me now,

let's not let this moment

go to waste

It is not the way

the trees sway,

it is not the way

you hold me close,

it is not the way

you would've chose,

it is not the way

you would pray,

it is not the way

my heart froze,

it is not the way

you chose to slay

Yesterday at Tatte, I saw you, well, fragments
of you, as I watched the baker knead the dough,
I saw your strength, he had your eyes and
that mischievous smirk, the same one you used to
win me over.
You went too soon. I stand here surrounded by
memories of our first date, it was this exact spot
where we first met. I stood on the black tile,
you stood on the white. You asked me my name and
my order, to which I replied, "Chelsea, croissant."
I was at a loss for words, you pulled off the James Dean
look so well, you were as kind as could be.
"Nice to meet you Chelsea, croissant, do you mind
if I join you?"
I squeaked "no" as quiet as a mouse and yet you heard
it.
I'm so thankful you did.
We didn't get a happily ever after
Being loved by you for the briefest of time was
fantasy enough as I rest my hand on my swollen belly.
I know you'll always be near

The sun is shining and yet

my heart isn't happy

the moon shines

deep into my soul

trying to break my

reverie,

I'm lost,

there is no being found

I'm trying not to think of you and how
you deceived me into being yours,
it happened over and over again,
you would've thought I
learned my lesson
the first time,
but sadly, no
I'm still here
looking for a way out

The fog crept in slowly
inching closer and closer
towards me,
it enveloped my whole being
without my permission

I knew this was the end

You loved me with a love
I couldn't quite comprehend,
you told me your love
would never fade
and yet, little by little
you slowly slipped away,
you told me I was childish,
and yet you were the one
to throw a fit when you
didn't get your way,
you took complete control
of me,
you were a monster

I didn't know you, but I was loved by you.

Falling deep into the abyss,
I thought I had lost all the
courage within me,
but there is a measly ounce left,

I am determined to never let it go

I was stressed and worried
and yet you held me in
your loving arms
you saved me,
how can I ever
repay you?

The tranquility never slumbers,

the daydreams never cease,

peace has a hold over me,

I hope it never lets me go

Fall has finally arrived
I have eagerly awaited its
appearance for a while now
the hollow branches,
the pumpkin patches,
the crisp air,
the nights we share
Fall, I'm so glad you're here

Bitterness lingers deep within my soul

I've tried to let it go

but no matter what I do

it stays,

from its dungeon

it holds me captive

Our souls connected by a mere glance

generations of writers and

yet here we are

passing each other

on this bridge

who are your favorites?

Hemingway, Longfellow

you seem to embody

the spirit of Hemingway,

but I'll never know

writer to writer, any advice?

your whisper barely reaches

my ear,

"write, as if it's the last time"

I thought I knew you,
but I didn't,
you thought you knew me,
but you didn't,
our world's torn apart
by yesteryear's news
a cello plays eerily
in the background
applauding our demise
can our love ever be
recovered?
we both shake our heads no
we stand and glance into each
other's souls one last time
and walk in different directions

My abuelita's worn hands

knead the masa dough

the wooden table is

covered with bowls of

every size and shape

I watch and listen

closely, as she shows

me step by step

what to do

this process takes hours

but there's no place

I'd rather be

at this table

with her making tamales

I sit here enveloped in a cashmere sweater
and yet I feel hopelessly alone,
my espresso sits untouched,
my legs feel the brunt of the
crisp, autumn air
I casually glance to my
left and to my right
everyone else seems so lonely,
we may be only a few feet
apart from each other
but we're in entirely different worlds

I've wandered my whole life searching for you,

waiting for a single indication that you're

here somewhere and that I haven't

dreamt up your existence,

perhaps I've met you before in a dream,

or a nightmare,

maybe I haven't met you at all,

maybe you don't exist,

maybe I'll never know

My soul has found its muse
deep in the forest
where the moss meets the wind
where the caterpillar meets the
fallen log,
where the lightning bug meets the sky,
my soul convenes with its muse in the
heart of the forest,
where the east converges with the west,
where the wildflowers whisper
to each other right there...
do you see it?

The day was beautiful until you spoke,

your words swept the sun behind the clouds,

they pulled the calm sea into angry waves,

sparrows fell from the sky,

you might want to rethink

voicing your thoughts next time,

you never know the catastrophe

that may ensue

Words have failed me,

my writer's blood has stopped flowing,

my inspiration left

without explanation,

I am but a skeleton without bones,

a bird without wings,

a tree without roots,

my world has spun out of orbit,

is it ever to be reclaimed?

Grief is a never-ending web we weave,

when we fear for our life,

when we mull over giving up,

when we give in to temptation,

the soul's grief continues to grow,

until an explosion is bound to occur,

don't let it possess your soul

The fear that followed that blissful day

was unmatched,

the world's cruelties lagged

deeper in my shadows

that fateful day,

left me stranded, alone, with no one to turn to,

the stars took everything from me

if I only had but one more

moment to tell you,

I love you

The cosmic dust surrounded
us last night,
intertwined in this very moment,
swaying to and fro
connected like never before,
the stars shine brightly for us,
guiding us home

Deep down, beneath the surface

I'm damaged,

some may even say broken,

I don't deserve love,

I wouldn't even know what it looked like,

what it felt like,

the hurt and pain have destroyed

a part of me,

never to be seen again

My mind is fierce,

trying to convince me to give up,

I'm determined to not let it dissuade me

from the hardships of life,

giving in is not an option

The crescent moon hung in the sky
suspended in daylight,
it radiated of happiness,
hope and new beginnings

Our love was never meant to last

and yet those first few years

were the best of my life,

those late nights you would

spin me around always brought me

back to the lake that special day,

the fog swirling just above

the water's surface,

our silence moved mountains,

with the snap of a twig,

you were gone,

forever

You were my first crush,
my first everything,
one simple question
and our love tore apart,
I should've never lashed out,
all these years later
I still think about you
and what could have been...
do you do the same?

No matter what happens,

we can still dream

here in these moments

I chose selfishness
over pity,
I chose to hurt
over heal,
I was wrong
and yet so thankful
for friends who forgive

Why is it a secret you wish to keep?

when we...

there used to be so much power behind those

two words

and now they're meaningless,

you knew the power you had over me

and not it's gone,

you're gone,

well, not completely

You consumed almost every part of me
a long time ago,
you still have an iron grip on my thoughts,
my soul,
please, I beg of you,
let me go

Does anyone care or simply unaware?

abandoned, alone

invitations declined,

excuses made,

will they ever change?

I must keep going without them.

Time is looming above me,
I feel the silent refrains from the
church bells,
tick, tock
tick, tock

The golden fields beckon me closer now,

they were hesitant to accept me

after what I had seen,

crows flew over the still body,

blood-stained hands loom below me,

it was like a dream,

but this was reality

the wheat glistened and rattled,

welcoming and forbidding me

at the same time.

The whispers seek me out,
they call upon my soul
waiting for me to answer
they tell me of a yesteryear
that I don't remember
and never will,
they call me Cassandra,
who is she?

As I sit in this dreary meadow,

the rain falls onto my skin,

my dearest hope is that

the raindrops may wash

away my many sorrows

The silence was thick,
deafening even,
I wanted to run away and hide
I was trapped,
until I made my escape
plausible

Snow fell gracefully from the sky

reminding me of hope

and a fresh start,

it was almost enough to put

my mind at ease,

the euphoria it caused was

surely welcome

Our souls were never meant for each other,
and yet you act as though I am yours,
I never have been
and never will be,
please, erase me from your memory,
forget you ever knew me

Your words pierced my soul,
how could you say such things?
did you not take my heart
into consideration?
oh, but you never intended
for me to find out...

My soul has not known
the weariness you speak of,
it knows something far greater...

...death

Fear has captured
my soul,
and yet I have hope

74

The mysteries of yesteryear
bore a travesty on my soul,
memories faded in the blink
of an eye,
corpses reunited

You haunt my dreams
in a grisly reverie,
you make demands
I cannot keep,
you are the demon
that taunts me at night

Though the weeks have passed
at a lion's rate,
we're still here amidst
this predicament,
as if no time has passed,
I wish I could make
it all go away,
but I can't,
you can't

Hello moon,
it's been a while,
I felt lost without you
I'm so glad you're back,
please don't let it be
so long next time...
although maybe you never left,
maybe I was too preoccupied
with things that don't matter,
my eyes were downcast
when I should've been
on the lookout for you,
you may have waited patiently for me,
I'm here hoping to never
lose sight of you again

I sit here waiting for you,

like waiting for the tea kettle to roar,

hoping and praying

your arrival doesn't

utterly scare me,

any moment,

you could appear

and upend my life forever,

which may not be a bad thing...

I'm alone with my thoughts
and no one else's,
it's a scary place to be

Jealousy doesn't become you,
flowers wilt at your words
you think you are safe
in the tower,
but terror is about to befall

I noticed the longing in your eyes,

is that why you left?

Broken doesn't begin to describe me,
I constantly wonder if
healing is a possibility

You have yet to find me,

I have yet to find you

our paths have not crossed lately,

I wonder about where you are,

what you are doing at this

very moment,

the shirt you are wearing,

the sidewalk you are using,

wondering if you are on your way

to find me,

or the local café next to our favorite

bookstore,

where we first met

Perhaps we are not destined
for each other after all,
what is "destined" anyway?
does it have to do with the
heat I feel in your gaze?
or the way we gravitate toward each other?
maybe that's all in my imagination...
do you feel it too?
my head says I'm done,
my heart whispers "not yet"

When I feel your eyes on me,

my world stops,

I freeze under your gaze,

my back straightens,

my thoughts suspended in time

when we lock eyes,

I wonder why you're looking at me in such a way,

do you think I'm strange?

is something on my face?

do you like me?

I feel this electricity between us,

am I the only one that feels it?

you stare deep into my soul,

what do you see?

does it scare you?

it scares me in the best way,

I long for the next time

our eyes meet,

do you?

Why do Sunday afternoons creep by
so slowly?
My mind chooses these lazy moments to
remind me of a daunting fact
Am I truly one good for one thing?
Is that why I may never find love?
I'm broken,
in the quietness, my mind becomes
the ultimate playground

She stood on the Ponts des Arts

overlooking the Seine,

her lips twitched as the

harsh wind blew in,

she tugged her trench coat closer

around her petite frame,

her eyes scanned the skyline,

filled with immeasurable hope,

she set off toward the Louvre,

feeling free and proud,

she was expectant of her

Parisian future

Alone I stood on this foreign trod,
besotted with my grief,
caring for no release
neighbors too kind to this
poor old soul,
turning a blind eye was my role,
silence was required of me,
for I could never mention
what happened in the sea

Emily Barrus

As the summer sun set slowly
over the horizon,
the seagulls skim the surface
of the water,
dancing to and fro
in the air,
my toes bury deeper in the sand,
as I pull my sweater over my shoulders,
I dream about those who have come here
before me,
couples holding hands,
kids flying kites
chasing each other,
pleading with their parents for ice cream,
the older man walking his dog,
people will come and go,
but this seascape
remains for those
who care to savor it

The light and dark danced

in a cosmic array of beauty,

for a moment, everything

felt tranquil,

and yet everything felt so vile,

how could these two

meet with no contention?

this peace was never

going to last,

but for an instant,

there was an unrealistic hope

There he is just beyond the
forest floor,
he lurks in the dense fog
watching and waiting
for the perfect moment
to distract, so the
strange creatures who
own him
may take their sweet
time hunting their prey

You were your only concern,
and yet you left your worth in the
pockets of others,
never did a moment pass
without seeking
validation,
the crumbs thrown your way
were devoured with
a vengeance,
is change on the horizon
for someone like you?

Emily Barrus

The Mirror

You see disgust,

I see beauty,

you see tangles of chaos,

I see luscious locks,

you see a revolting red hue,

I see porcelain perfection,

what you and I see

are vastly different,

you look into me every day

searching for more

than I can give,

I'm a mere reflection,

hoping you see yourself as

beautiful as I do

The chill of the night

breaks my reverie,

my mind drifting off

the past,

bitter memories at

the forefront

dreary meadows,

broken lullabies,

birds chirping to

their demise,

foggy pastures beckon me

like you did,

cunningly wicked,

devilishly tempting,

moments better to

be forgotten

Emily Barrus

The willow trees sway,

the woodpeckers furiously peck,

the sun shines gloriously

across the land,

spring is here

indulging us in its beauty,

the blue jay flies from

branch to branch,

the daffodils stand proudly,

a beautiful spring day charms us

with its presence,

birds chirping a cheery hello,

nature beckons us to

linger a moment longer

Bonds were severed long ago,
familiar ties no matter,
you could care less about
blood relation,
you treat us like scum
what did we ever do to
deserve this?
nothing,
we only had open hearts and
homes to give,
it's your loss upon rejecting,
the damage is done
you may never change,
that's ok,
we've lived a lovely life
without you

Emily Barrus

The old stone house

sat untouched,

secrets buried deep within,

the ivy manicured

so perfectly,

rotten trees creaked

with the wind,

the rose bushes bare,

the petals crushed into the earth,

the curse had prevailed

no one dared step

foot on the premises,

until yesterday,

never to be seen again

Wings are what lift me up,
when nothing else can
today's troubles and tomorrows
sorrows will fade,
they are but the cycle of life,
I'd prefer to stay in my cocoon, but that
is no longer an option
opinions, judgements,
I will rise,
no matter what's thrown my way
I will rise,
the butterfly will rise

There's beauty in the slowness,

the mundane,

it may be harder to find at times, we just

need to lean in and

look a little closer,

as the bird flies overhead

watch its grace, its beauty,

the flower stands proudly, eager

to be admired,

its beauty astounding,

there's beauty in the rain,

in the mess,

in the quibbles and squabbles

There's a quiet stillness in the morning...
the birds chirp a cheery welcome,
the clouds hang in the sky with
no sign of moving any time soon,
the leaves sway quietly on the
gentle breeze,
glancing upward quickly to see
a robin with a worm between its beak,
the world is not yet awake,
it seems like anything is possible
at this hour

Is it truly meant to be
love like a canopy
fully engrossing my soul
from my head to my toes
looking up to the stars
wishing near and far
boldness a necessity
reality, a simple remedy
for what is possible
believing I was made
for you, and you for me
waiting for the moment
when our paths cross,
today or tomorrow?
we may never know
be alert and be ready
when the time comes
the heart won't know
what hit it

At the top of a villa,

an old man stood

peering over the landscape,

the vines, the waves

harsh memories remembered

wishing they could be buried

as easily as they had been formed

yesteryear, felt like mere moments

ago and another life

all at the same time,

lost loves, broken bonds

hearts crushed as easily

as the grapes in this very field

he is still blamed for another man's doing

and yet no one believes him,

if you ever visit Bonassola,

look east and you may catch a glimpse of him

The Grapevine

Shallow roots grow deeper
and deeper into the earth,
the thin trunk weaves itself upward,
curving branches stretch every which way
the buds slowly form into the
perfect green bulbs
the leaves ferociously huge
I sit here waiting for the grapes to ripen
they still have about a month to go
trying to be ever so patient
I admire its tenacity for it keeps
growing no matter what

Moments in the Garden

The cooling breeze is certainly welcome,
leaves rustling,
the smell of peppermint and dill
entice my senses,
the cat perched on leftover brick
swishes its tail stirring dead, rust
colored leaves, the white butterfly
makes its splendid appearance
amongst the greenery
clovers and weeds are resilient
the sun peeking through the clouds
for the briefest of moments
I yearn for the cool breeze
the moment it disappears
the plane overhead breaks my reverie,
the breeze is back and for that I'm
eternally grateful
I smile as a swallowtail flies by
my day is made in these simple moments

Looking out the window across the meadow,

such ferocious feelings arise,

of repine and sublime at the same time

I wish for the birds' freedom,

the butterfly's beauty,

to be a wildflower

amidst the darkest storm,

locked in this tower

with nothing to devour

what is the point?

I cannot breathe without others staring,

my life a mere play

for others to enjoy,

these moments at the window

are my only source of joy

The damp coolness of the morning
entices me to look further into the stillness
the woodland creatures
carry on their merry way
the dark soil tells of its richness,
life carries on,
the hawk continues to swirl above,
bunnies hopping quietly
to nearby shelter
wild berries push through
the earth and thrive,
precisely where they're meant to be
the dew providing nourishment
the sun shines gloriously
welcoming a new day

Mossy trees enveloped me
are now my forever home,
the forest welcomed me,
warned me,
my soul begging for nature's secrets
I promised to keep them close
monstrous noises seeking to scare me
only planted my being further
in the forest floor
I was made of something stronger
something I didn't quite know
here amidst the ferns and fungi
is where I would find out

I wish to be like a butterfly
that flies from flower to flower
no humanly cares or sorrows
always looks forward to tomorrow
its beauty purely for others enjoyment
the freedom to fly anywhere at any moment
but how did it get here?
the caterpillar gloriously
transformed into something
even more beautiful
to be like a butterfly
sounds rather divine,
doesn't it?

The stench of your betrayal still

plagues me even after a decade of

major loss and upheaval

my feelings never mattered to you,

not in the beginning,

not when you declared your love,

a dingy dungeon is what you deserve,

no, you deserve far worse

but knowing your luck

that probably won't happen,

how many others have you betrayed?

someone must have severely

hurt you a long time ago,

being hurt is no excuse

for what you did

The door creaked loudly as we entered the antique store,

every crook and crevice filled to the brim

with beautiful, quirky vintage pieces

my dad points to a typewriter by the window,

the sun's rays hitting it just right

I glance at the price tag

there's no way we'll be leaving this behind,

on the beautiful drive home,

we pass a spot on the Lafayette Trail

once home, we put the typewriter to the test

with a cup of tea steeping,

I place my fingertips on the keys and start to type

I quickly realize this is nothing like a computer

keyboard. My mother then shows me how it's done.

I look in wonder at this antique and imagine those

who may have used this from yesteryear

I think of the literary greats from my home state

did Dickinson, Alcott or Emerson use a typewriter

in their later writing years? Or perhaps, it was too strange

from pen and paper. While we may never know, the

inspiration starts to flow and the typing begins...

Emily Barrus

By the seaside, I seek clarity,

with anxious anticipation I nestle in

the sand and close my eyes,

listening to the waves gently roll

I feel closest to God by the water

I can feel His presence here

the wind wraps its arms around

me like a fierce hug

never letting me go

I'm reminded of my

wonderful Savior

and His never-ending love

Late night melodies pierce my soul

I yearn to be near You

so many worldly distractions

start to creep in

You are all that my soul thirsts for

You are all that I need

please, Lord, help me

break this cycle,

give me strength to resist

these snares that fight

against me

less of the world,

more of You,

You, forever, always

Emily Barrus

The wind ferociously pounded against

my back as I stood facing my favorite place,

Corn Cove,

the bluffs stand majestically

looming above me

the dense fog

starts to eerily roll in,

the waves churn wildly

crashing on the sandy beach,

as day turns into night

the tempest's fury deepens

there's beauty in the rugged chaos,

the unknown,

here at the sea everything seems magical

hope rises within me, anything is possible

I bury my toes into the damp sand

watching a hermit crab in

shallow water,

seagulls soar above me

here, even amidst the rough waters

I cherish these simple moments,

I never want to leave

The fog descended slowly on the
cool morning,
leaves swirling slowly to the ground
a raven circles overhead
a new day promptly turns deadly,
the sound of scrawny branches
creaking eerily surrounds me,
there in the darkness,
a low growl emerges
shall I try to make a hasty retreat
or accept my fate?

Emily Barrus

The Moon & I

The moon was my light in the darkness

my guiding light to all that is good

in the world

peering at its brightness,

I felt seen,

it knows me

and I know it,

my reason for making it this far

gone in an instant

craters hold the darkest secrets

their trust not easily broken

I yearn for my guiding light to return,

amidst the waiting,

every night I search the sky

expectant,

filled with overwhelming hope,

knowing someday soon,

we will meet again

Yellows, oranges and reds
surround us,
awe and wonderment
consume our souls
oh, what vast beauty!
how can it be?
loving Lord
such as thee
created this
for you and me

Emily Barrus

The Unknown

Darkness surrounds me
life's trials slowly start to
suffocate my whole being
I yearn to know what's ahead on
this lifelong journey
plagued with doubts and fear?
the war on my mind rages
does it get any better?
the unknown is terrifying
how will I make it through
the storms that will surely
come?
You
You will see me through
You are with me in every unknown

You met me there in Trafalgar Square
with but a penny to your name
the overwhelming shame
cast the deepest of shadows
on that frigid night
surrounded by twinkle lights
no matter your station
this was our ill fate,
jolly moments
vastly turning gray,
regret has never known your name,
what a pity,
the new horizon is up ahead

Why am I here?

what is my purpose?

would anyone care if I wasn't

here tomorrow?

these thoughts keep swirling

and yet I'm reminded

God

God has me here for a reason

His opinion is the only one that matters

as long as there is

breath in my lungs,

I'll keep going

You are beautiful,
no matter what they say
you are beautiful,
don't listen to the hate

Like the bee,

this rejection stings,

before word was received

hope soared higher than

the tallest mountain peak

this old soul was crushed

for but a moment,

life goes on,

there's no time to worry

about what isn't meant to be

keep going,

your time will come

Shriveled in the chaos

of right and not so

the weathered tendrils

wrap their knotty way through the

fiercest of nights

the harshest of blizzards

no match,

hardy, determined,

able to withstand

the trying times sure to come

daring us to do the same,

stand strong

when temptation to falter creeps in,

with a relentless grip,

hold on

Pain is not always visible

the inner scars

marring life's present and future

not to be defined

forever

a broken, yet beautiful reminder,

keep going,

always keeping the beauty

of the reminder at hand

Peering deep into the darkness,

no light in this dungeon

the sudden realization

there wasn't a choice

moment by moment

forced deeper into the cage,

pushed,

suffocated,

tormented

belief in anything wearing thin

the slightest crack of light shines

in hope filling the barren crevices

a new beginning

within the faintest of reaches at night,

the moonlight pours in slowly the

cracks stretch, escape is possible

dawn approaches

not a moment to waste

freedom to be claimed

Hustle and bustle too much, rest
running ragged from errands, rest
a floury, frosting mess baking
dozens of cookies, rest
fingers numb from writing
Christmas cards, rest
wrapping paper strewn about,
gifts piling higher, rest,
calendar brimming with every
holiday activity, rest
snow falling beautifully, rest
fireplace crackling, rest
family safely snuggled in bed, rest
reflecting on God's blessings, rest
God loves you and me, rest
knowing the reason for the season,
rest in Him

A New Dawn

Darkness overwhelms the deepest
depths of the soul
pasts, pains, bound in chains
horrid memories, shaken to the core
trying to forget, a mere impossibility
this mound of flesh
broken,
bruised, scars
an unwelcome reminder
yet, beauty is found here
amidst the jagged edges
once full of repine,
a new dawn is breaking
light filling the cracks and crevices
the brokenness is not forever
little by little
molded into a masterpiece
no longer overwhelmed by the dark
radiating new light

Worldly woes surround me
more and more they pile on
heart distressing
fatigue compressing
seeking the smallest sliver of hope
looking to the sky
small white snowflakes
fall gracefully
for a mere moment
blink and you'll miss it
ponder these joy-filled winks
such virtue is found in the
tiniest of pieces

The first few snowflakes fell today
gracefully winding down to the
frozen earth below, the white glimmering
specks a welcome of hope in this
dreary world, Christmas time is here
carols sung with utmost cheer,
oranges and cloves strewn throughout
a delicious smell wafting,
the last few leaves hang on for dear life
the wind carries them up with a fury
the landscape settled with barren trees
our Savior offers an unwavering peace
the sparce, the cold, stories untold
no match for our Creator, He
blankets the seasons with hope and love
it's not hard to find, look to Him
these wintry moments will pass
in a hurry, each new day filled with
possibility, our greatest comfort
being held in His loving arms
no matter what befalls us,
He will never let go

Emily Barrus

Twinkling lights ne're in sight
in this dreary town,
paper boys scurry as the church
bells ring, the postman whistles
cheery tunes, snow falls lightly
candles glow brightly
children hurry to the sweets shop
pennies jingling in their pockets
Christmas makes this town come alive
it's almost here
bend an ear to the sky
sleigh bells faintly
draw closer

Why sudden emotion
filling me with sadness?
I feel so far away from You
these moments
I feel so alone
glimmers of hope
enlighten this heart
maybe the tiny
slivers will
someday be complete

These selfish thoughts run
me ragged,
how do I stop?
I want to free myself
of this burden
loving others is what You ask
please help
work in the weary soul

This tiny teacup brings me joy
adorned in beautiful colors
the vessel with little room to be filled
taking joy in simple things
not much room is required
a small dose of a good thing
makes this heart soar
my Lord, my God
how I think of You
You are my mainstay,
my Bread of Life,
my Living Water
You are able to do vast with
the tiniest of offerings,
may my life honor You
may what little I have to offer be
used by Your mighty power

Frosty, chunky snowflakes fall

tenderly from the sky

gleaming in the celeste,

the mundane

head tilted upward

ready to welcome the sweet

drops of winter

their beauty brings hope and light

to many this season

gone in but a moment

cherishing what was and what could be

the chill,

the thrill,

the wonder,

hold these wintry moments close

a sure treasure to store in this

beating heart

awaiting its beautiful return

The glow of the streetlight
shines like a halo on
this dreary night
rain pouring from the sky
no other noise is evident
Christmas lights illuminate
the darkness
there is beauty to be
found amidst the bleak
see the Christmas tree through
the window?
keep these moments close
hope is found here

These anxious nerves cripple me

it's of my own volition

run ragged,

mind racing

I'm letting the enemy win

hope misplaced

trust erased

how do I give it all to You?

oh, Lord! I beg of You

please help me!

With you...
the last place I thought
I'd find myself
tears stain every page
tables tossed
plates shattered
how did we get here?
is there anything
left for us?
hope seems to have diminished
long ago,
the moment you stole my heart

Seeking after that
which I cannot find
I am all but blind
mysteries, histories
a new year about to unfold
memories to be
stored forever in this heart
candles burning,
snow falling,
melodies sung with cheer
through the year
look ahead,
there is beauty to behold

Peering into the looking glass
I see my reflection before me
the day is still
not a sound to be heard
this isn't like most Christmases
the wilderness solemn
reprieve calms my heart
chilled to the bone,
sun peeking through
the clouds
shadowed with doubt
the dew clinging on
for dear life
shall I do the same?

Emily Barrus

Pieces of Heaven fall from the sky

this winter wonderland

beckons me closer

the quiet air,

the chickadee's prayer

chilled to the bone

this is my home

bare branches no longer

frosty windowpanes

snuff out the biting breeze

hearts aglow

hot cocoa on the stove

the hearth a welcome reprieve

blanketed in white

no end in sight

the truest treat for the soul

Crochet away

the pain,

the shame,

the tears,

the cares

thread the needle

gliding back and forth

keep moving

creating this piece of art

life slipping away

don't worry

don't rush

take your time

the beauty is worth the wait

Emily Barrus

Cobblestone streets

take a leap

ivy frames the doorway

there's nothing like the night

air in Rome

take a seat

enjoy a momentary retreat

twirl the pasta

savor its delicious power

raise a glass

catch someone's eye

anything is possible on a night in Rome

music playing, merrymaking

where strangers become friends

wishing this night never ends

alleys filled with tourists like you and me

tiramisu or gelato, why choose?

life has never felt so good

passing the Spanish Steps, barely out of breath

embrace this moment, cherish this one life

life is beautiful on this night in Rome

Amsterdam to Tipperary

no need to catch the ferry

sit back and watch

the world pass below you

adventure never-ending

jump on the plane

you won't regret these days

strolling through the countryside

or reveling the taste of a stroopwafel

no time to waste

you decide your fate

what will you choose

before it's too late?

Dust off your wings

it's time to fly

and soar to unknown heights

the world is scary,

but don't be wary

I'm right by your side

when you're ready

lift your wings...

...and rise

Thank you for reading

♥ Emily

Emily Barrus is a writer who loves traveling, reading and enjoying God's creation. She is a published poet and author. She has found healing through writing and seeks to be an encouragement to those who read her writing. She currently resides in Massachusetts.